@theresetgroup

 @therealreset

 www.theresetgroup.com

 The Reset Group

We are a group of licensed mental health professionals who work with top tier athletes, coaches, organizations, churches, and families to develop the winning mindset of leaders to overcome mental blocks in all areas of life.

ARE YOU READY FOR A BREAKTHROUGH?
We do life coaching for individuals struggling with depression, anxiety, life transitions, and couples who are fighting for their marriage. Contact us for more information at www.theresetgroup.com/take-action

Speaking inquiries email us at joe@theresetgroup.com

*For my wife, Kristin and our children Sawyer and Avonlea. You cannot reset your mindset without family.*

*–Joe*


*To my parents, Mary and Joe, for endless support during my playing days and to my husband, Rich, and our children, Joaquin and Lyncoln, who support and value my work as a coach.*

*–Priscilla*

## 30 Days of Mental Training for WHOLE Athletes

***Welcome RESET athlete!*** We are excited for you to join the RESET journaling movement with our **30 Day RESET Journal**. WHOLE athletes are people who train their body, mind and emotions in order to perform at the highest levels on and off the playing arena.

In case you didn't already know, journaling is a powerful mindset tool. Research in this area supports that journaling not only helps clarify your thoughts and feelings by writing them out, it can help reduce cortisol levels (the stress hormone), lead to more effective problem solving skills, resolve conflicts and promote healthy forms of communication with others such as those found in team environments.

This journal contains 30 days of prompts and daily routines used by our professional and collegiate athletes to make them mentally elite in their sport. We believe that investing just 1% of your day *(that's 14 minutes each day)* on your mindset through performance journaling can help train your mind and develop the habits you need to get a competitive edge in your sport and give you valuable life skill too.

**The RESET Group**
Joe Jardine
NCAA/NFL Performance Mindset Coach

Priscilla Tallman
NCAA Performance Mindset Coach

Your **30 Day RESET Journal** contains a Pre-Game Huddle, 28 days of journal pages, and a Post-Game Huddle for a total of 30 days. The seventh day of each week ends with a **RECAP**. After the completion of week 4 you will be prompted to complete the Post-Game Huddle.

The **Pre and Post-Game Huddle** are assessments that will measure your mindset growth throughout the 30 days. Before starting "Day 1", fill out the Pre-Game Huddle assessment. Be as honest as you can. If you don't understand a question, leave it blank or guess what you think it might mean and enter your score. After "Day 28", complete the Post-Game Huddle assessment at the end of the journal. Compare the first assessment to the second one and see if there are improvements or areas in which you feel you have grown. Are there certain areas in which you would like to do more work? Is there anything that stayed the same or where no growth occurred? Tracking these areas may help you to become more self-aware of your process and own the parts where more work is needed.

A daily routine is very important in the development of your performance mindset. Routine primes confidence and success. *Routine re-sets the mind-set.* For the rest of your career, develop a routine on how you approach practices and the game. Set it and stick with it.

Each day contains a **DAILY RESET** with three components to be completed before your journal prompt.

Practicing your daily reset will help begin to shift your mind from the negative to the positive. You are training your brain to look at the strengths and not the deficits of yourself as an athlete.

1:  **Self-Evaluation** — Learning how to accurately and honestly assess our emotions on any given day is a valuable life skill that creates self-awareness. Each day, start by identifying your emotional state. If you score less than a 6, it is encouraged you share that with a coach or healthy adult.

2:  **3-2-1 Journaling** — We have to train our minds to begin each day from a place of abundance and gratitude. Gratitude creates an emotional shift from the inside out, but it takes daily practice to see things we may otherwise overlook.

3:  **Visualization** — rehearsing a great practice or acquisition of skill is a great tool to making it happen and minimize anxiety in the moment.

# TABLE OF CONTENTS

*Rate yourself for each question below using this scale:*

**1**    **2**    **3**    **4**    **5**

*needs work*    *meh*    *its fine*    *good*    *great!*

Rate your attitude as an athlete.    _____

Rate your effort as an athlete.    _____

Rate your openness to feedback.    _____

Rate your application of feedback.    _____

Rate your openness to ask questions.    _____

Rate your pre-practice physical preparation.    _____

Rate your pre-game physical  preparation.    _____

Rate your pre-practice mental preparation.    _____

Rate your pre-game mental preparation.    _____

Rate your openness to learn something new.    _____

Rate your overall performance as an athlete.    _____

*developing your*
# MINDSET

Where is your brain?
*That's right, it's inside your head.*

Where are your muscles?
*That's right, they're inside your body.*

Some athletes make the mistake and think that mindset or mental work is done separately from the physical aspects of your sport, but your body and mind work together - they are literally in the same space - therefore mindset work IS your sport.

Answer these questions: *What type of athlete do you want to be? What daily decisions does that athlete possess? What habits does that athlete possess?* Decisions become habits and habits become systems. In fact, *"we do not rise to the level of our goals, we fall to the level of our systems"* –James Clear, Atomic Habits.

## THEREFORE, YOUR MINDSET IS A CHOICE.

When you create healthy daily habits you free up valuable brain power and energy to learn technical aspects of your sport - and that's how you develop your mindset.

# DAILY RESET – MINDSET

 **Rate Yourself.** On a scale of 1-10
*(1 = low mood, hopeless / 10 = great mood)*
rate your overall mood today. Emotional self affects your
performance, so self awareness in this area is important.

**Write your score: _____ / 10**

 **3-2-1 Journaling**
*3 things* you are *grateful for*

_____

_____

_____

*2 things* you are *excited about*

_____

_____

*1 thing* you want to *accomplish* for yourself today

_____

 **Visualize.** Spend 5 minutes visualizing what you want to
accomplish at practice or in your game today. Find a quiet
spot, close your eyes and rehearse this intention.

## HOW DO I FEEL TODAY? *(circle the emoji(s) that apply)*

**NEXT LEVEL:** *Write the corresponding feeling underneath the emoji(s) you circled.*

# DAILY RESET – MINDSET

 **Rate Yourself.** On a scale of 1-10
*(1 = low mood, hopeless / 10 = great mood)*
rate your overall mood today. Emotional self affects your
performance, so self awareness in this area is important.

**Write your score:** _____ / 10

 **3-2-1 Journaling**
*3 things* you are *grateful for*

_____

_____

_____

*2 things* you are *excited about*

_____

_____

*1 thing* you want to *accomplish* for yourself today

_____

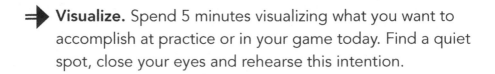 **Visualize.** Spend 5 minutes visualizing what you want to
accomplish at practice or in your game today. Find a quiet
spot, close your eyes and rehearse this intention.

Our support system, or the people who surround and support us daily, are an important part of our success on and off the field. List below the people who fit that role in your life.

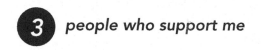

*people who support me*

_____

_____

_____

*people who hold me accountable*

_____

_____

*person who comforts me when I'm struggling*

_____

# DAILY RESET – MINDSET

 **Rate Yourself.** On a scale of 1-10
*(1 = low mood, hopeless / 10 = great mood)*
rate your overall mood today. Emotional self affects your
performance, so self awareness in this area is important.

**Write your score: _____ / 10**

 **3-2-1 Journaling**
*3 things* you are *grateful for*

_____

_____

_____

*2 things* you are *excited about*

_____

_____

*1 thing* you want to *accomplish* for yourself today

_____

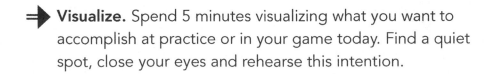 **Visualize.** Spend 5 minutes visualizing what you want to
accomplish at practice or in your game today. Find a quiet
spot, close your eyes and rehearse this intention.

*"It's not the will to win that matters, everyone has that. It's the will to prepare to win that matters,"*
*Paul "Bear" Bryant*

 ***things I can do to prepare myself mentally for practice***

_____

_____

_____

 ***things I can do to prepare myself physically for practice***

_____

_____

 ***thing I can do to prepare myself emotionally for practice***

_____

# DAILY RESET – MINDSET

➡️ **Rate Yourself.** On a scale of 1-10
*(1 = low mood, hopeless / 10 = great mood)*
rate your overall mood today. Emotional self affects your
performance, so self awareness in this area is important.

**Write your score:** \_\_\_\_\_ / 10

➡️ **3-2-1 Journaling**
*3 things* you are *grateful for*

_____

_____

_____

*2 things* you are *excited about*

_____

_____

*1 thing* you want to *accomplish* for yourself today

_____

➡️ **Visualize.** Spend 5 minutes visualizing what you want to
accomplish at practice or in your game today. Find a quiet
spot, close your eyes and rehearse this intention.

*"Your results are the product of either personal focus or personal distractions. The choice is yours,"*
*John Di Lemme*

 **productive activities that lift my mood when I'm down**

_____

_____

_____

 **productive activities I can do when I feel bored**

_____

_____

 **activity I can do to serve/help someone else today**

_____

# DAILY RESET – MINDSET

**➡ Rate Yourself.** On a scale of 1-10
*(1 = low mood, hopeless / 10 = great mood)*
rate your overall mood today. Emotional self affects your
performance, so self awareness in this area is important.

**Write your score: _____ / 10**


**➡ 3-2-1 Journaling**
*3 things* you are *grateful for*

_____

_____

_____


*2 things* you are *excited about*

_____

_____


*1 thing* you want to *accomplish* for yourself today

_____

**➡ Visualize.** Spend 5 minutes visualizing what you want to
accomplish at practice or in your game today. Find a quiet
spot, close your eyes and rehearse this intention.

It is important for us to know the difference between where we can go to recharge or rest and where we go that distracts us.

 *places I can go to recharge my "batteries"*

_____

_____

_____

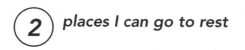 *places I can go to rest*

_____

_____

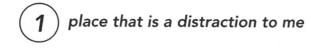 *place that is a distraction to me*

_____

**NEXT LEVEL:** *Rest and recovery are important life skills. Tear out this page and tape it to a visible place you see every day as a reminder of the ways you can find rest and avoid distractions.*

# DAILY RESET – MINDSET

 **Rate Yourself.** On a scale of 1-10
*(1 = low mood, hopeless / 10 = great mood)*
rate your overall mood today. Emotional self affects your
performance, so self awareness in this area is important.

**Write your score: _____ / 10**

 **3-2-1 Journaling**
*3 things* you are *grateful for*

_____

_____

_____

*2 things* you are *excited about*

_____

_____

*1 thing* you want to *accomplish* for yourself today

_____

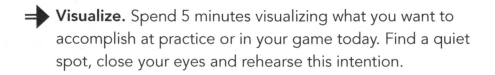 **Visualize.** Spend 5 minutes visualizing what you want to
accomplish at practice or in your game today. Find a quiet
spot, close your eyes and rehearse this intention.

## THE LAUNCH EQUATION

**Cognitive Behavioral (or Cog-B) Theory** in psychology is the go to tool for behavior change. One of the basic tenets is that our THOUGHTS drive our BEHAVIOR. The LAUNCH equation is rooted in Cog-B and helps us identify something learned that we can launch in the next practice. It is within the process of giving ourselves feedback where learning takes place.

1: Identify one thing you *LEARNED* today.

2: Identify one thing you can *ADJUST* for next time.

3: How will you train, practice, or *LAUNCH* the adjustment?

$$\underline{\hspace{3cm}} + \underline{\hspace{3cm}} = \underline{\hspace{3cm}}$$
*(learn)*        *(adjust)*        *(launch)*

# DAILY RESET – MINDSET

 **Rate Yourself.** On a scale of 1-10
*(1 = low mood, hopeless / 10 = great mood)*
rate your overall mood today. Emotional self affects your
performance, so self awareness in this area is important.

**Write your score: _____ / 10**


**3-2-1 Journaling**
*3 things* you are *grateful for*

_____

_____

_____

*2 things* you are *excited about*

_____

_____

*1 thing* you want to *accomplish* for yourself today

_____

**Visualize.** Spend 5 minutes visualizing what you want to
accomplish at practice or in your game today. Find a quiet
spot, close your eyes and rehearse this intention.

# RECAP - MINDSET
*(circle any that apply or add your own)*

## What did I **do well** this week?

| | | |
|---|---|---|
| my attitude | was a good teammate | showed up |
| my effort | open to feedback | set practice goals |
| patience | good communication | had manners |
| a certain skill | helped setup/teardown | |
| | asked good questions | |

_____

_____

## What needs **improving**?

| | | |
|---|---|---|
| my attitude | a certain skill | recover from a mistake |
| my effort | understand rules | reframe a mistake |
| listen to coach | understand drill | |
| support a teammate | asking a question | |

_____

_____

## What will **I bring** to the next practice or game?

| | | |
|---|---|---|
| attitude to learn | a certain skill | reframe a mistake |
| my best effort | a good question | be open to feedback |
| listen to coach | a practice goal | patience |
| support a teammate | help setup/teardown | communication |

_____

_____

*defining your*
# GOALS

**Goal setting** is merely **intention setting.**

As you progress from making decisions that become habits, you now have the foundation to set intentions and those intentions will help you reach your goals.

Goal setting answers these questions:

> *What do I intend to accomplish for this practice?*
>
> *What do we intend to accomplish as a team?*
>
> *How do I intend to contribute my gifts for the good of the team?*

When you set a goal, you have to take it from words on a paper to action steps that get you and your team closer to where you want to be.

# DAILY RESET – GOALS

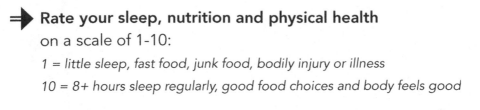 **Rate your sleep, nutrition and physical health**
on a scale of 1-10:
*1 = little sleep, fast food, junk food, bodily injury or illness*
*10 = 8+ hours sleep regularly, good food choices and body feels good*

**Write your score: _____ / 10**

➡ **3-2-1 Journaling**

*3 **great choices** I can make today*

_____

_____

_____

*2 **ways** I can promote **better health***

_____

_____

*1 **way** I can keep my body feeling **physically prepared**
for my sport*

_____

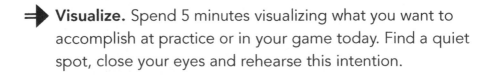 **Visualize.** Spend 5 minutes visualizing what you want to
accomplish at practice or in your game today. Find a quiet
spot, close your eyes and rehearse this intention.

Fill the bubble with some

## *WILD, CRAZY, BIG GOALS*

you have.

# DAILY RESET – GOALS

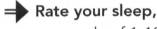

 **Rate your sleep, nutrition and physical health**
on a scale of 1-10:

*1 = little sleep, fast food, junk food, bodily injury or illness*

*10 = 8+ hours sleep regularly, good food choices and body feels good*

**Write your score:** _____ / 10

 **3-2-1 Journaling**

**3 great choices** *I can make today*

_____

_____

_____

**2 ways** *I can promote* **better health**

_____

_____

**1 way** *I can keep my body feeling* **physically prepared**
*for my sport*

_____

 **Visualize.** Spend 5 minutes visualizing what you want to
accomplish at practice or in your game today. Find a quiet
spot, close your eyes and rehearse this intention.

Goals rarely make a straight line from point A to point B. **Draw in** what it might look like to set a goal and meet it.

●
**A**

●
**B**

What are some common road blocks or barriers that can cause setbacks when pursuing your goal?

_____

_____

_____

_____

# DAILY RESET – GOALS

 **Rate your sleep, nutrition and physical health**
on a scale of 1-10:

*1 = little sleep, fast food, junk food, bodily injury or illness*

*10 = 8+ hours sleep regularly, good food choices and body feels good*

**Write your score: _____ / 10**

 **3-2-1 Journaling**

*3 great choices* I can make today

_____

_____

_____

*2 ways* I can promote **better health**

_____

_____

*1 way* I can keep my body feeling **physically prepared**
for my sport

_____

 **Visualize.** Spend 5 minutes visualizing what you want to
accomplish at practice or in your game today. Find a quiet
spot, close your eyes and rehearse this intention.

What are some things I feel when my goals seem out of reach?
**Circle as many** as you feel appropriate or add your own.

- AFRAID
- ANGRY
- FRUSTRATED
- CLOSED OFF
- ENCOURAGED
- BURNED OUT
- EXHAUSTED

- DISCOURAGED
- MAD
- SAD
- DISAPPOINTED
- LIKE BLAMING SOMEONE
- LIKE I LET SOMEONE DOWN

- DETERMINED
- HOPELESS
- LIKE QUITTING
- PERSISTENT
- RESILIENT
- SICK

_____   _____

_____   _____

Write down your **top three** here.

1. _____

2. _____

3. _____

# DAILY RESET – GOALS

 **Rate your sleep, nutrition and physical health**
on a scale of 1-10:

*1 = little sleep, fast food, junk food, bodily injury or illness*

*10 = 8+ hours sleep regularly, good food choices and body feels good*

**Write your score:** _____ / 10

➡ **3-2-1 Journaling**

*3 great choices* I can make today

_____

_____

_____

*2 ways* I can promote *better health*

_____

_____

*1 way* I can keep my body feeling *physically prepared*
for my sport

_____

 **Visualize.** Spend 5 minutes visualizing what you want to accomplish at practice or in your game today. Find a quiet spot, close your eyes and rehearse this intention.

Think about the first time you shot a layup, served a ball, swung a bat, caught a pop fly or took off from the starting blocks. You didn't get it on your first try did you? No, your coach or a teammate likely broke down the skill into smaller parts. Goals can work that way too.

In the table below, write down one goal and three steps that will help you achieve that goal. Pick something specific and tangible, avoid things like "be better at …"

*Example: Goal = Eat nutritious food that fuels me,*
*3 Steps = choose a vegetable for one meal, pack a piece of fruit in my bag,*
*choose water instead of soda, juice or energy drinks.*

| GOAL | 3 STEP ACTION PLAN |
|---|---|
|  | 1. |
|  | 2. |
|  | 3. |

**NEXT LEVEL:** *Pick one goal and complete the 1st step in the 3 step action plan today*

# DAILY RESET – GOALS

**Rate your sleep, nutrition and physical health**
on a scale of 1-10:

*1 = little sleep, fast food, junk food, bodily injury or illness*

*10 = 8+ hours sleep regularly, good food choices and body feels good*

**Write your score: _____ / 10**

**3-2-1 Journaling**

*3 **great choices** I can make today*

_____

_____

_____

*2 **ways** I can promote **better health***

_____

_____

*1 **way** I can keep my body feeling **physically prepared**
for my sport*

_____

**Visualize.** Spend 5 minutes visualizing what you want to accomplish at practice or in your game today. Find a quiet spot, close your eyes and rehearse this intention.

You can only work on **THREE** things at your next practice. What **THREE** things will help you reach one of your personal or team goals?

1. _____

   _____

2. _____

   _____

3. _____

   _____

**NEXT LEVEL:** *Tell a coach, teammate or family member what you are working on.*

# DAILY RESET – GOALS

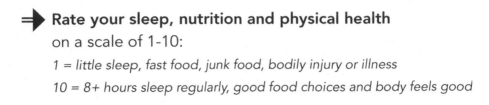 **Rate your sleep, nutrition and physical health**
on a scale of 1-10:

*1 = little sleep, fast food, junk food, bodily injury or illness*

*10 = 8+ hours sleep regularly, good food choices and body feels good*

**Write your score: _____ / 10**

 **3-2-1 Journaling**

*3 great choices I can make today*

_____

_____

_____

*2 ways I can promote better health*

_____

_____

*1 way I can keep my body feeling physically prepared
for my sport*

_____

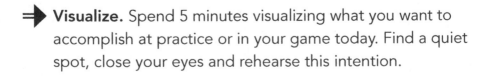 **Visualize.** Spend 5 minutes visualizing what you want to
accomplish at practice or in your game today. Find a quiet
spot, close your eyes and rehearse this intention.

Distractions aren't just things that happen on the field, they are circumstances, conflicts or adversities that can happen at any point in your life. For instance, a tough financial situation in your family can be a distraction. So can academic stress, friend drama, social media, parental conflict, peer pressure and many other things.

What are **THREE** things that might serve as a distraction to your goals?

1. _____

   _____

2. _____

   _____

3. _____

   _____

**NEXT LEVEL:** *Acknowledging these distractions won't make them go away, but writing them down can help us start the conversation with ourselves and then others. Everyone has distractions, those of us who acknowledge them can learn how to ask for help when we need it.*

# DAILY RESET – GOALS

 **Rate your sleep, nutrition and physical health**
on a scale of 1-10:

*1 = little sleep, fast food, junk food, bodily injury or illness*

*10 = 8+ hours sleep regularly, good food choices and body feels good*

**Write your score: _____ / 10**

 **3-2-1 Journaling**

*3 **great choices** I can make today*

_____

_____

_____

*2 **ways** I can promote **better health***

_____

_____

*1 **way** I can keep my body feeling **physically prepared**
for my sport*

_____

 **Visualize.** Spend 5 minutes visualizing what you want to accomplish at practice or in your game today. Find a quiet spot, close your eyes and rehearse this intention.

# RECAP - GOALS

How did I **work on my mindset** this week?
*(e.g. journaling, gratitude, meditating or taking down time)*

_____

_____

_____

When is the best time to work on my mental training?

| | |
|---|---|
| MORNING | BETWEEN CLASSES |
| BEFORE SCHOOL | AFTER SCHOOL |
| AFTERNOON | BEFORE BED |
| BEFORE PRACTICE | AFTER PRACTICE |
| TRAINING ROOM | OTHER _____ |

The most helpful part of journaling is:

_____

_____

_____

*developing your*
# com·mu·ni·ca·tion

Your brain has a relationship with words. How you speak to yourself is an important part of shaping your story as an athlete.When the story is off it can get in the way of your performance and limits your ability to hear feedback from your coaches or teammates.

Fear, anxiety, confidence and happiness are influenced by words.

> *The words you say can either be*
>
> **motivating or deflating**
>
> *to you and your teammates.*

One big area we can work on communicating to ourselves or others is looking at how we respond to mistakes or failure.

# DAILY RESET – COMMUNICATION

 **Rate your self talk** on a scale of 1-10

*1 = negative self talk, beating myself up over a mistake or swearing loudly*

*10 = bouncing back from a mistake, self talk reflects the process, not the result*

**Write your score:** _____ / 10

**➡ 3-2-1 Journaling** *(vary your answers for each day)*
   ***3 ways*** *I can* ***encourage a teammate*** *today*
   *(pick a different teammate each day this week)*

_____

_____

_____

   ***2 ways*** *I can* ***practice healthy self talk***
   *(e.g. process oriented vs. result oriented)*

_____

_____

   ***1 helpful thing*** *I can tell myself before my next practice or game*

_____

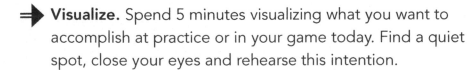 **Visualize.** Spend 5 minutes visualizing what you want to accomplish at practice or in your game today. Find a quiet spot, close your eyes and rehearse this intention.

What are some *healthy ways* my teammates communicate with me?

1. _____

2. _____

3. _____

What are some *healthy ways* I communicate with my teammates and coaches?

1. _____

2. _____

3. _____

# DAILY RESET – COMMUNICATION

 **Rate your self talk** on a scale of 1-10

*1 = negative self talk, beating myself up over a mistake or swearing loudly*

*10 = bouncing back from a mistake, self talk reflects the process, not the result*

**Write your score: _____ / 10**

➡ **3-2-1 Journaling** *(vary your answers for each day)*
**3 ways** I can **encourage a teammate** today
*(pick a different teammate each day this week)*

_____

_____

_____

**2 ways** I can **practice healthy self talk**
*(e.g. process oriented vs. result oriented)*

_____

_____

**1 helpful thing** I can tell myself before my next practice or game

_____

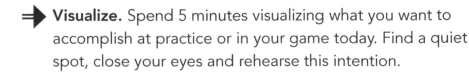 **Visualize.** Spend 5 minutes visualizing what you want to accomplish at practice or in your game today. Find a quiet spot, close your eyes and rehearse this intention.

**Nonverbal communication (or body language) can send big messages.** List some healthy and not so healthy forms of non-verbal communication.

healthy

not healthy

**NEXT LEVEL:** *Circle one of the healthy non-verbal communication ways you listed that you want to practice this week. What does it look like in practice? Competition?*

# DAILY RESET – COMMUNICATION

 **Rate your self talk** on a scale of 1-10

*1 = negative self talk, beating myself up over a mistake or swearing loudly*

*10 = bouncing back from a mistake, self talk reflects the process, not the result*

**Write your score: _____ / 10**

 **3-2-1 Journaling** *(vary your answers for each day)*

**3 ways** *I can **encourage a teammate** today*
*(pick a different teammate each day this week)*

_____

_____

_____

**2 ways** *I can **practice healthy self talk***
*(e.g. process oriented vs. result oriented)*

_____

_____

**1 helpful thing** *I can tell myself before my next practice or game*

_____

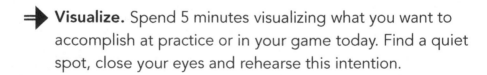 **Visualize.** Spend 5 minutes visualizing what you want to accomplish at practice or in your game today. Find a quiet spot, close your eyes and rehearse this intention.

**Our words matter.** What are some healthy and not so healthy ways our coaches or parents communicate with us during competition?

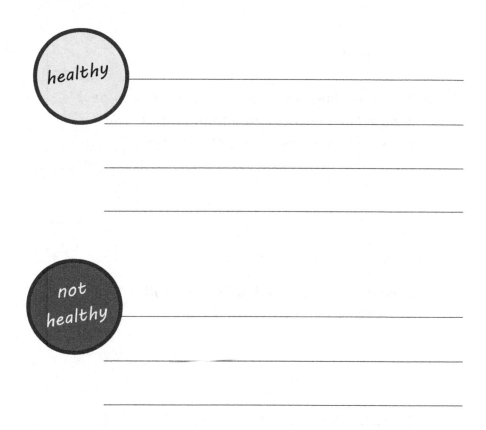

healthy

_____

_____

_____

_____

not
healthy

_____

_____

_____

_____

# DAILY RESET – COMMUNICATION

 **Rate your self talk** on a scale of 1-10

*1 = negative self talk, beating myself up over a mistake or swearing loudly*

*10 = bouncing back from a mistake, self talk reflects the process, not the result*

**Write your score: \_\_\_\_\_ / 10**

 **3-2-1 Journaling** *(vary your answers for each day)*

*3 ways I can encourage a teammate today*
*(pick a different teammate each day this week)*

_____

_____

_____

*2 ways I can practice healthy self talk*
*(e.g. process oriented vs. result oriented)*

_____

_____

*1 helpful thing I can tell myself before my next practice or game*

_____

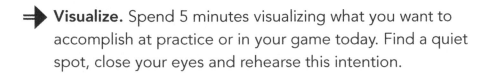 **Visualize.** Spend 5 minutes visualizing what you want to accomplish at practice or in your game today. Find a quiet spot, close your eyes and rehearse this intention.

*Leadership is revealed by how well you handle your mistakes and the mistakes of others.*

Things I **tell a teammate** after they make a mistake.

1. _____

_____

_____

2. _____

_____

_____

3. _____

_____

_____

# DAILY RESET – COMMUNICATION

 **Rate your self talk** on a scale of 1-10
*1 = negative self talk, beating myself up over a mistake or swearing loudly*
*10 = bouncing back from a mistake, self talk reflects the process, not the result*

**Write your score:** _____ / 10

➡ **3-2-1 Journaling** *(vary your answers for each day)*
**3 ways** *I can **encourage a teammate** today*
*(pick a different teammate each day this week)*

_____

_____

_____

**2 ways** *I can **practice healthy self talk***
*(e.g. process oriented vs. result oriented)*

_____

_____

**1 helpful thing** *I can tell myself before my next practice or game*

_____

➡ **Visualize.** Spend 5 minutes visualizing what you want to accomplish at practice or in your game today. Find a quiet spot, close your eyes and rehearse this intention.

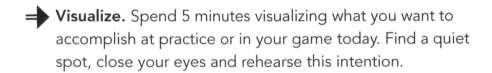

*Negative self-talk affects our ability to move on quickly from mistakes and reinforces thoughts about performance (e.g. fear, anger, shame).*

Things I tell **myself** after a mistake:

1. _____

_____

_____

2. _____

_____

_____

3. _____

_____

_____

**NEXT LEVEL:** *How does this self-talk differ from how I speak to a teammate? What if I spoke to myself the way I speak to others?*

# DAILY RESET – COMMUNICATION

➡️ **Rate your self talk** on a scale of 1-10

*1 = negative self talk, beating myself up over a mistake or swearing loudly*

*10 = bouncing back from a mistake, self talk reflects the process, not the result*

**Write your score:** _____ / 10

➡️ **3-2-1 Journaling** *(vary your answers for each day)*
**3 ways** I can **encourage a teammate** today
*(pick a different teammate each day this week)*

_____

_____

_____

**2 ways** I can **practice healthy self talk**
*(e.g. process oriented vs. result oriented)*

_____

_____

**1 helpful thing** I can tell myself before my next practice or game

_____

➡️ **Visualize.** Spend 5 minutes visualizing what you want to accomplish at practice or in your game today. Find a quiet spot, close your eyes and rehearse this intention.

***Thoughts drive behavior.*** The way we behave after a mistake affects our ability to learn and grow from them or our tendency to get stuck thinking about them.

Things I  DO  after I make a mistake.

1._____

2._____

3._____

4._____

### ARE THESE

○ ***Helpful*** to my progress

● ***Not so helpful*** to my progress

# DAILY RESET – COMMUNICATION

➡ **Rate your self talk** on a scale of 1-10

*1 = negative self talk, beating myself up over a mistake or swearing loudly*

*10 = bouncing back from a mistake, self talk reflects the process, not the result*

**Write your score: _____ / 10**

➡ **3-2-1 Journaling** *(vary your answers for each day)*
  **3 ways** I can **encourage a teammate** today
  *(pick a different teammate each day this week)*

_____

_____

_____

  **2 ways** I can **practice healthy self talk**
  *(e.g. process oriented vs. result oriented)*

_____

_____

  **1 helpful thing** I can tell myself before my next practice or game

_____

➡ **Visualize.** Spend 5 minutes visualizing what you want to accomplish at practice or in your game today. Find a quiet spot, close your eyes and rehearse this intention.

# RECAP – COMMUNICATION

**Look back at Day 18.** You wrote down things you tell a teammate after a mistake. Write them down here, but instead of directing those words at someone else, write them as if you are saying them to yourself.

_____

_____

_____

_____

Choose one of the above comments and **write it in ALL CAPS** here:

_____

_____

_____

_____

**This is your MANTRA.** Say this to yourself after a mistake, on a tough practice day, on a day you feel down or not motivated.

*taking*
# OWNERSHIP

Your practice is your process. How you use your time is up to you. One of the ways we take ownership of our practice is by **PREPARING** yourself physically, mentally and emotionally for your practice. This is not only a skill that will prepare you for your sport, but it will prepare you for a big test or project you have for school, a job interview, a recruiting visit or a tryout for a new team.

# DAILY RESET – OWNERSHIP

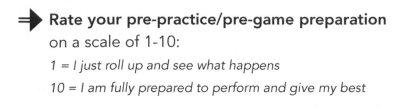 **Rate your pre-practice/pre-game preparation**
on a scale of 1-10:

*1 = I just roll up and see what happens*

*10 = I am fully prepared to perform and give my best*

**Write your score:** _____ / 10

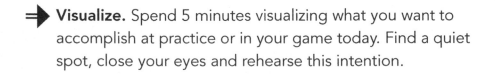 **3-2-1 Journaling**

**3 things my sport has allowed me to do**
*that I'm grateful for*

_____

_____

_____

**2 songs or quotes** *that put me in a great mood*

_____

_____

**1 person I can talk to** *before a game that
keeps me focused*

_____

➡ **Visualize.** Spend 5 minutes visualizing what you want to
accomplish at practice or in your game today. Find a quiet
spot, close your eyes and rehearse this intention.

1: Who are some athletes I **admire**?

_____

_____

_____

2: Why do I admire these athletes?

_____

_____

_____

3: What characteristics do they have that I'd like to have?

_____

_____

_____

**NEXT LEVEL:** _Look up a quote from an athlete that inspires you. Write it down where you can see it daily._

# DAILY RESET – OWNERSHIP

 **Rate your pre-practice/pre-game preparation**
on a scale of 1-10:

*1 = I just roll up and see what happens*

*10 = I am fully prepared to perform and give my best*

**Write your score:** _____ / 10

**3-2-1 Journaling**

*3 things my sport has allowed me to do*
that I'm grateful for

_____

_____

_____

*2 songs or quotes* that put me in a great mood

_____

_____

*1 person I can talk to* before a game that
keeps me focused

_____

**Visualize.** Spend 5 minutes visualizing what you want to
accomplish at practice or in your game today. Find a quiet
spot, close your eyes and rehearse this intention.

INSIDE the hand write five things I **CAN CONTROL** in practice/games.

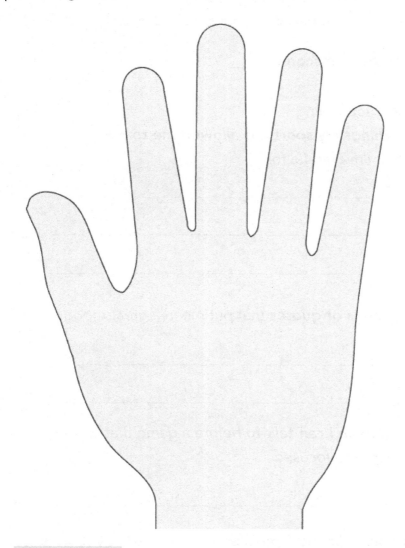

**NEXT LEVEL:** *Write your favorite ones on your hand for your next practice.*

# DAILY RESET – OWNERSHIP

 **Rate your pre-practice/pre-game preparation**
on a scale of 1-10:

*1 = I just roll up and see what happens*

*10 = I am fully prepared to perform and give my best*

**Write your score:** _____ / 10

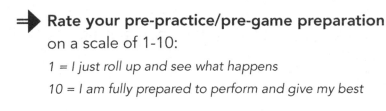 **3-2-1 Journaling**
   ***3 things my sport has allowed me to do***
   *that I'm grateful for*

_____

_____

_____

   ***2 songs or quotes*** *that put me in a great mood*

_____

_____

   ***1 person I can talk to*** *before a game that*
   *keeps me focused*

_____

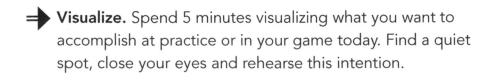 **Visualize.** Spend 5 minutes visualizing what you want to accomplish at practice or in your game today. Find a quiet spot, close your eyes and rehearse this intention.

OUTSIDE the hand, write  five things I **CANNOT CONTROL** in practice/games.

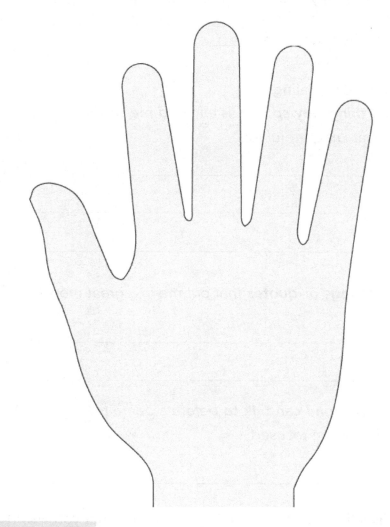

**NEXT LEVEL:** *Why do you think we wrote these things OUTSIDE of the hand?*

# DAILY RESET – OWNERSHIP

 **Rate your pre-practice/pre-game preparation**
on a scale of 1-10:

*1 = I just roll up and see what happens*

*10 = I am fully prepared to perform and give my best*

**Write your score:** _____ / 10

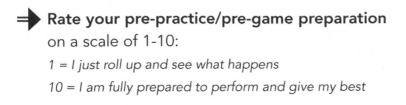 **3-2-1 Journaling**

**3 things my sport has allowed me to do**
that I'm grateful for

_____

_____

_____

**2 songs or quotes** *that put me in a great mood*

_____

_____

**1 person I can talk to** *before a game that*
*keeps me focused*

_____

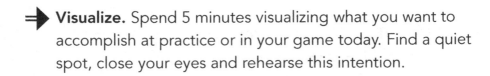 **Visualize.** Spend 5 minutes visualizing what you want to accomplish at practice or in your game today. Find a quiet spot, close your eyes and rehearse this intention.

You cannot control both sides of the scoreboard. The highest performers control their inner scoreboard and focus on what they *can* control.

In the **HOME** box, write your team name, team motto and favorite part of being on this team.

In the **AWAY** box, write two things you do to prepare for an AWAY contest or performance.

| HOME | AWAY |
| --- | --- |
|  |  |

# DAILY RESET – OWNERSHIP

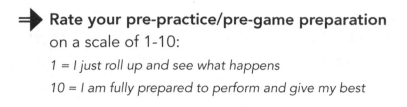 **Rate your pre-practice/pre-game preparation** on a scale of 1-10:

*1 = I just roll up and see what happens*

*10 = I am fully prepared to perform and give my best*

**Write your score:** _____ / 10

**3-2-1 Journaling**

**3 things my sport has allowed me to do** *that I'm grateful for*

_____

_____

_____

**2 songs or quotes** *that put me in a great mood*

_____

_____

**1 person I can talk to** *before a game that keeps me focused*

_____

**Visualize.** Spend 5 minutes visualizing what you want to accomplish at practice or in your game today. Find a quiet spot, close your eyes and rehearse this intention.

Visualize a **successful practice.**
What does this look like?

How did you prepare yourself for
this practice?

**NEXT LEVEL:** *Write the date when this practice will*

*happen next:* _____

# DAILY RESET – OWNERSHIP

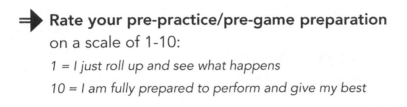 **Rate your pre-practice/pre-game preparation**
on a scale of 1-10:

*1 = I just roll up and see what happens*

*10 = I am fully prepared to perform and give my best*

**Write your score:** _____ / 10

 **3-2-1 Journaling**
**3 things my sport has allowed me to do**
*that I'm grateful for*

_____

_____

_____

**2 songs or quotes** *that put me in a great mood*

_____

_____

**1 person I can talk to** *before a game that*
*keeps me focused*

_____

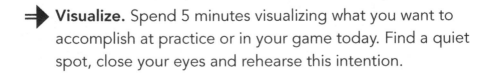 **Visualize.** Spend 5 minutes visualizing what you want to accomplish at practice or in your game today. Find a quiet spot, close your eyes and rehearse this intention.

Perhaps the best way to take ownership of your athletic experience is to understand **WHY** you play your sport. Your **WHY** is rooted in your value systems. Whether you are aware of it or not, you make decisions every day based on your value system. If you know what those values are, you can focus and execute on them daily. If you do not, you will adopt values from social media, your peers, or whomever you decide to follow that particular day. Circle some of the values that are most important to you:

| | | |
|---|---|---|
| FAITH | LEARNING | LOYALTY |
| INTENTIONALITY | REPUTATION | DEPENDABILITY |
| DETERMINATION | KNOWLEDGE | ACHIEVEMENT |
| PERSEVERANCE | GROWTH | AUTHENTICITY |
| WORK ETHIC | HONOR | COMMITMENT |
| JOYFULNESS | GRACE | FAME |
| FUN | TRUST | FRIENDSHIPS |
| GRATITUDE | INTEGRITY | POPULARITY |
| ABUNDANCE | TEAMWORK | STABILITY |
| ENTHUSIASM | ENJOYMENT | WEALTH |
| | IDENTITY | |

# DAILY RESET – OWNERSHIP

 **Rate your pre-practice/pre-game preparation**
on a scale of 1-10:

*1 = I just roll up and see what happens*

*10 = I am fully prepared to perform and give my best*

**Write your score:** _____ / 10

 **3-2-1 Journaling**

*3 things my sport has allowed me to do*
that I'm grateful for

_____

_____

_____

*2 songs or quotes* that put me in a great mood

_____

_____

*1 person I can talk to* before a game that
keeps me focused

_____

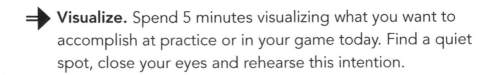 **Visualize.** Spend 5 minutes visualizing what you want to accomplish at practice or in your game today. Find a quiet spot, close your eyes and rehearse this intention.

## RECAP – OWNERSHIP

Write down **3 reasons WHY** you play your sport:

Write down **three FEARS** you have about playing your sport:

As mentioned on Day 27, our **WHY** is rooted in our value system (you circled several that are important to you). Our **FEARS** on the other hand are often rooted in shame or guilt. When we ignore our fears, they can become stumbling blocks to performing our best. Though many think otherwise, sharing your fears is NOT a weakness - it's a ***super power***.

Fill in the following equation with **>** or **<**

**My WHY is _____ My FEAR**

*Now that you've completed your 30 days of journaling, re-rate yourself for each question using the scale below. Did any of your scores change? If so, what and why?*

| 1 | 2 | 3 | 4 | 5 |
|---|---|---|---|---|
| needs work | meh | its fine | good | great! |

Rate your attitude as an athlete. _____

Rate your effort as an athlete. _____

Rate your openness to feedback. _____

Rate your application of feedback. _____

Rate your openness to ask questions. _____

Rate your pre-practice physical preparation. _____

Rate your pre-game physical  preparation. _____

Rate your pre-practice mental preparation. _____

Rate your pre-game mental preparation. _____

Rate your openness to learn something new. _____

Rate your overall performance as an athlete. _____

Information for this appendix has been compiled and created as a source for client education in a clinical setting and may contain research and references from "Social Psychology" by David G Myers & Jean M Twenge.

This appendix is not a diagnostic tool. If you or someone you know have a life threatening situation or need immediate medical help, call your doctor or dial 911.

# DEPRESSION

### *What are the symptoms of depression?*

- Depressed mood or sadness most of the time

- Lack of energy

- Inability to enjoy things that used to bring pleasure

- Withdrawal from friends and family

- Irritability, anger, or anxiety

- Inability to concentrate

- Significant weight loss or gain

- Significant change in sleep patterns (inability to fall asleep, stay asleep, or get up in the morning)

- Feelings of guilt or worthlessness

- Aches and pains (with no known medical cause)

- Pessimism and indifference (not caring about anything in the present or future)

- Thoughts of death or suicide

When someone has five or more of these symptoms more often than not for two weeks or longer, that person is probably depressed.

### How is depression different from regular sadness?

Everyone has some ups and downs, and sadness is a natural emotion. The normal stresses of life can lead anyone to feel sad every once in a while. Things like an argument with a friend or spouse, loss of a job, life transitions such as moving or getting a new job or starting a new school, not being chosen for a team, or a best friend moving out of town can lead to feelings of sadness, disappointment, or grief. These reactions are usually brief and go away with a little time and care.

Depression is more than occasionally feeling blue, sad, or down in the dumps, though. Depression is a strong mood involving sadness, discouragement, despair, or hopelessness that lasts for an extended period of time. It interferes with a person's ability to participate in normal activities.

Depression affects a person's thoughts, outlook, and behavior as well as mood. In addition to a depressed mood, a person with depression may feel tired, irritable, and notice changes in appetite. When someone has depression, it can cloud everything. The world looks bleak and the person's thoughts reflect that hopelessness. Depression tends to create negative and self-critical thoughts. Because of feelings of sadness and low energy, those with depression may pull away from those around them or from activities they once enjoyed. This usually makes them feel more lonely and isolated, worsening their condition. Depression can be mild or severe. At its worst, depression can create such feelings of despair that a person contemplates suicide.

## Why does one become depressed?

There is no single cause for depression. Many factors play a role including genetics, life events, family and social environment and medical conditions.

**Genetics:** Research shows that some individuals inherit genes that make it more likely for them to get depressed. However, not everyone who has the genetic makeup for depression becomes depressed, and many who have no family history of depression have the condition.

**Life Events:** The death of a family member, friend, or pet can sometimes go beyond normal grief and lead to depression. Other difficult life events, such as when parents divorce, separate, or remarry, can trigger depression. Even events like moving or changing schools can be emotionally challenging enough that a person becomes depressed.

**Family and Social Environment:** A negative, stressful, or unhappy family atmosphere can have a negative effect on one's self-esteem and lead to depression. This can also include high-stress living situations such as poverty, homelessness, or violence. Substance abuse could cause chemical changes in the brain that negatively impact mood. The damaging social and personal consequences of substance abuse can also lead to depression.

**Medical Conditions:** Certain medical conditions can affect hormone balance and therefore lead to depression. When these medical conditions are diagnosed and treated by a doctor, the depression usually disappears. For some, undiagnosed learning disabilities might block school, work or relationship success, hormonal changes might affect mood, or physical illnesses might present challenges or setbacks.

### How do I get help?

Depression is one of the most common emotional problems around the world. The good news is that it's also one of the most treatable conditions. Those who get help for their depression have a better quality of life and enjoy themselves in ways that they weren't able to before.

Treatment for depression can include psychotherapy, medication, or a combination of both. Psychotherapy with a mental health professional is very effective in treating depression. Therapy sessions can help one understand more about why they feel depressed and learn ways to combat it. Sometimes, doctors prescribe medicine for a patient with depression. It can take a few weeks before that person feels the medicine working. Because every person's brain is different, what works well for one person might not work for another.

Everyone can benefit from mood-boosting activities like exercise, yoga, dance, journaling, or art. It can also help to keep busy no matter how tired you feel.

Those who are depressed shouldn't wait around hoping it will go away on its own; depression can be effectively treated. Others may need to step in if someone seems severely depressed and isn't getting help.

Many find that it helps to open up to others including friends, family or other individuals they trust. Simply saying, "I've been feeling really down lately and I think I'm depressed," can be a good way to begin the discussion. Ask to arrange an appointment with a therapist. For teens, if a parent or family member can't help, turn to a school counselor, best friend, or a helpline.

# ANXIETY

### Introduction to Anxiety

Generalized Anxiety Disorder or GAD is characterized by excessive, exaggerated anxiety about everyday life events. People with symptoms of GAD tend to always expect disaster and can't stop worrying about health, money, family, work, or school. These worries are often unrealistic or out of proportion for the situation. Daily life becomes a constant state of unease, fear, and dread. Eventually, the anxiety so dominates the person's thinking that it interferes with daily functioning.

### What is anxiety?

Anxiety is a natural human reaction that serves an important basic survival function. It acts as an alarm system that is activated whenever a person perceives danger. When the body reacts to a potential threat, a person feels physical sensations of anxiety: a faster heartbeat and breath rate, tensed muscles, sweaty palms, nausea, and trembling hands or legs. These sensations are part of the body's fight-flight response, which is caused by a rush of adrenaline and other chemicals. This reaction prepares the body to make a quick decision to either stay and fight that threat or try to escape from it (fight or flight). It takes a few seconds longer for the thinking part of the brain (the cortex) to process the situation and evaluate whether the threat is real, and if it is, how to handle it. If the cortex sends the all-clear signal, the fight-flight response is deactivated and the nervous system can relax. If the brain reasons that a threat might last, feelings of anxiety and the physical symptoms listed above may linger, keeping the person alert.

### *What are the symptoms of generalized anxiety disorder?*

GAD affects the way a person thinks, but the anxiety can lead to physical symptoms as well. Symptoms of GAD include:

- Excessive, ongoing worry and tension
- An unrealistic view of problems
- Restlessness or a feeling of being "edgy"
- Irritability
- Muscle tension
- Headaches
- Sweating
- Difficulty concentrating
- Nausea
- The need to go to the bathroom frequently
- Tiredness
- Trouble falling or staying asleep
- Trembling
- Being easily startled
- Other anxiety disorders (such as panic disorder, obsessive-compulsive disorder and phobias)
- Depression
- Drug/alcohol abuse

### What causes generalized anxiety disorder?

Although the exact cause of GAD is not known, a number of factors, including genetics, brain chemistry, and environmental stressors appear to contribute to its development.

**Genetics:** Some research suggests that family history plays a part in increasing the likelihood that a person will develop GAD. This means that the tendency to develop GAD may be passed on in families.

**Brain chemistry:** GAD has been associated with abnormal levels of certain neurotransmitters in the brain. Neurotransmitters are special chemical messengers that help move information between nerve cells. If the neurotransmitters are out of balance, messages cannot travel through the brain properly. This can alter the way the brain reacts in certain situations, leading to anxiety.

**Environmental factors:** Trauma and stressful events, such as abuse, the death of a loved one, divorce, or changing jobs or schools may lead to GAD. The use of and withdrawal from addictive substances, including alcohol, caffeine, and nicotine, could also worsen anxiety.

### How are anxiety disorders treated?

Anxiety disorders can be treated by both mental health professionals and therapists. A therapist can look at the symptoms someone is dealing with, diagnose the specific anxiety disorder, and create a plan to help the person get relief.

A particular type of talk therapy called cognitive-behavior therapy (CBT) is often used. In CBT, a person learns new ways to think and act in situations that can cause anxiety, and to manage and deal with stress. The therapist provides support and guidance and teaches new coping skills such as relaxation techniques or breathing exercises. Sometimes, but not always, medication is used as part of the treatment for anxiety.

### *How common is generalized anxiety disorder?*

About 4 million American adults suffer from GAD during the course of a year. It most often begins in childhood or adolescence, but can begin in adulthood. It is more common in women than in men.

# HOW TO WIN THE NIGHT

Here are our go to's if you are struggling to fall asleep or stay asleep.

***Setting yourself up for a good night's rest:***

- Create a nightly routine (taking a shower or bath, put on soft music, dim the lights).

- Start the process of preparing for sleep an hour before.

- Go to bed the same time every night.

- Turn off all electronics and/or put the phone face down.

***Trouble falling asleep or going back to sleep:***

- Reflect on your blessings and what you are grateful for.

- Count backwards from 100.

- Have a notepad next to your bed to write down any pending to do's or thoughts.

- Relax your body by telling your body to go to sleep, starting with your toes and going up to your head.

- After 30 minutes of not being able to fall asleep, get up and do something and then return to your bed.

# SUICIDE IDEATION

If you are having suicidal thoughts connect with someone as soon as possible, whether that be a professional, a family member, a friend, or a significant other. Tell them what you are thinking and feeling. Call the suicide hotline 1-800-784-2433 for additional support. For the next 24 hours do not be alone. If you have thoughts, a plan, and means of harming yourself dial 911 or go to your local hospital immediately.

# PANIC/ANXIETY ATTACK

Choose one or all of the following, whatever works best for you:

- **Squeeze ice or hold a cold drink.**
  *IMPORTANCE: This cools down your CNS (Central Nervous System) and redirects your thoughts onto the coldness of the ice instead of focusing on your anxious thoughts*

- **Breathe in through your nose and blow out through pierced lips to maximize your oxygen levels.**
  *IMPORTANCE: Your lungs trap oxygen during the time of an attack and this helps you get your oxygen out while at the same time maximizing the oxygen levels in your body.*

- **Get outside. Go for a walk and as you walk shift your eyes from left to right.**

*IMPORTANCE: This gets your body moving and back in control of your body. Fresh air is a good change of environment. When you move your eyes from left to right it brings tranquility to the brain.*

• **Say the following mantra over and over again, "God is in control, I am okay. I am okay, God is in control."** *IMPORTANCE: This gets your mind focused off yourself and gives you positive self-talk.*

• **Practice grounding exercises using your five senses.** What do you hear, see, smell, taste, or feel around you? IMPORTANCE: Activating your five senses will help bring you into the here and now.

## COPING SKILLS AND DEFENSIVE MECHANISMS

**Defense Mechanisms:** Unhealthy ways we respond to our thoughts and emotions.

**Coping Skills:** Healthy ways we respond to our thoughts and emotions.

| DEFENSE MECHANISMS | COPING SKILLS |
|---|---|
| Avoiding responsibilities | Practice deep breathing |
| Blaming others | Positive Self-Talk |
| Denial of problems | "Stinkin'Thinkin'" worksheet |
| Catastrophizing problems | Share your need |
| Displacement –<br>    transferring emotions onto<br>    other innocent things or people | Exercise |
| | Journal |
| | Listen to music |
| Day dreaming | Squeeze ice |
| Acting out/Throwing a tantrum | Pray |
| Become controlling | Write what you are thankful for |
| Repression | Read scriptures |
| Yelling | Take a bath or shower |
| Projecting | Interact with your pet (if applicable) |
| Cutting | Eat a healthy snack |
| Over/Under eating | Go for a drive |
| Over sleeping | Read a book |
| Substance abuse | Do a puzzle |
| Sarcasm/Humor | Write, draw, paint, photography |
| Regression | Play an instrument, sing, dance, act |
| Passive Aggressiveness | Do some gardening |
| Victimization | Watch a good movie |
| Comparison | Play a board/card game |
| Going shopping | Clean or organize your environment |
| | Lower your expectations of the situation |
| | Keep an inspirational quote with you |
| | Scream in a pillow |
| | Punch a pillow |
| | Cry |
| | Laugh |

## Notes

———— Notes ————

——————— Notes ———————

—————— Notes ——————

Thank you for completing the **30 Day RESET Journal**! We hope you were able to see the value of daily journaling as a habit and continue the practice throughout your athletic journey. Journaling is part of becoming self-aware as an athlete. Self-awareness helps us see our blind spots and allows us to move forward in strength and power. When we do not acknowledge areas where we get stuck or where we feel alone as athletes, it affects our performance on the field as well as friendships and relationships off the field. Sports is likely a big part of your life, but it's not the only part of your life. We appreciate your willingness to grow and learn with us!

**The RESET Group**
**Joe Jardine, MFT**
**Priscilla Tallman MS, Clinical Psychology**

**Share your feedback with us!**
> **Instagram:**@theresetgroup
> **Twitter:** @therealreset
> **email:** joe@theresetgroup.com

## The RESET Group

**Joe Jardine** is a performance mindset coach for elite athletes and coaches in the NFL and NCAA. He is privileged to work with athletes and coaches from several organizations including the Dallas Cowboys, Detroit Lions, LA Rams, USC, CAL, UCLA, Northwestern, Notre Dame and more. Joe has a private practice in Orange County California and is a Sports Psychology Professor at Vanguard University.

**Priscilla Tallman** works with NCAA athletes as a Performance Mindset Coach and coaches PAC 12 Beach Volleyball. Tallman's athletic career includes First Team All-America honors and All-SEC honors all four years at UGA including Freshman of the Year in 1991 and Player of the Year in 1994. Tallman also played two tours with the USA National Team in 1994 and 1995, a season of professional volleyball in Geneva, Switzerland and in 2006 was inducted into the University of Georgia's prestigious Circle of Honor.

**www.theresetgroup.com**      @theresetgroup

 @therealreset     f The RESET Group

*Mindset journal design by Esther BeLer Wodrich.*
*www.estherbeler.com*

Made in the USA
Coppell, TX
16 August 2020